TRY THIS!

FREAKY PHYSICS EXPERIMENTS FOR THE MAD SCIENTIST IN YOU

KAREN ROMANO YOUNG

PHOTOGRAPHS BY MATTHEW RAKOLA

NATIONAL GEOGRAPHIC

WASHINGTON, D.C.

WEIRDPHYSICS

sn't life strange? Maybe you don't think so now, but you'll KNOW so after trying the activities in this chapter. Open your mouth and say "Awe!"

BIKE WHEEL GYROSCOPE PART 1

WALKING ON EGGS

MYO GIANT AIR CANNON

BIKE WHEEL GYROSCOPE PART 2

MYO GIANT AIR CANNON

Have a blast (of air)!

CONCEPTS

FLUID DYNAMICS, BERNOULLI'S
PRINCIPLE, CONSERVATION OF ENERGY

HOW LONG IT TAKES
one hour

WHAT YOU NEED
20- or 30-gallon (77- or 98-L) plastic
trash can
clear plastic shower curtain
bungee cord
scissors or craft knife
optional: paper cups, colored smoke
balls (also called smoke bombs)

Bernoulli's principle applies to:
• putting "spin" on a table-tennis ball or a tennis ball (using uneven pressure to do it)
• "bending" a soccer ball with that same spin, as David Beckham famously did
• spraying a water hose by pinching it
• this air cannon

"That is majestically glorious."
—Stephanie

QUESTION THIS!

• What's the maximum distance at which your air cannon will work to knock down the cup or blow back someone's hair?

WHAT TO DO

1 WITH ADULT supervision, use the craft knife to cut a circle six to eight inches (15 to 20 cm) in diameter in the bottom center of the trash can. Note: Often these cans have a circle in the center. Just cut out that circle.

2 STRETCH THE SHOWER curtain material across the open top end of the trash can and fasten it with a bungee cord. Use scissors to trim the excess shower curtain, leaving three or four inches (8 to 10 cm) hanging below the bungee cord.

3 TO WORK THE AIR cannon, lift the trash can by one handle and hold it horizontally over your shoulder or against your hip. Give the shower curtain membrane a sharp pat in the center.

> **WHAT TO EXPECT** When you pat the shower curtain, a puff of air should come out of the opening at the bottom end. You can set up the cups as a target and practice shooting the air at them to knock them over. Or see if a friend notices the puff of air hitting him.

> **WHAT'S GOING ON?** Bernoulli's principle explains what happens when you pinch a garden hose to make water squirt out. When you narrow the hose, you create a vortex, which makes the fluid at the center of the flow move faster than the fluid along the edges. So the water's velocity increases as its pressure decreases. In the air cannon, the same principle applies to air that is pushed unevenly through the hole in the trash can.

"Quit shooting air at me!"
—Patsy

BONUS

SMOKE RINGS

You can blow smoke rings with your air cannon, using colored smoke from a smoke bomb. Do this outside! Have an adult set the smoke bomb and light it. Place the hole of your air cannon over the smoke bomb, and let the air cannon sit until it fills with colored smoke. Lift the cannon and pat the membrane to blow a smoke ring.

BIKE WHEEL GYROSCOPE
PART 1

How does a bicycle stay up?

This experiment helps you see how a bicycle works. If you've ever tried to see how slowly you can pedal before you lose your balance, you've already experimented with the principles explored here.

WHAT TO DO

1 ATTACH THE BICYCLE pegs to each side of the wheel's axis. This gives you a way to hold the wheel so that it can spin freely.

2 TIE THE CLOTHESLINE firmly to one side of the axle, between the peg and the wheel.

3 SUSPEND THE BICYCLE wheel by the cord from an overhang or doorway. We used a nail in the beam at the top of the porch. You can tie it, but we had a friend hold the end of the clothesline to just keep it hung firmly over the nail.

4 SPIN THE WHEEL as fast as you can.

> GLITCH? Wheel won't spin? If your line is too thick, it can impede the spinning. Try thinner clothesline.

> WHAT TO EXPECT When spinning, the wheel should hang not exactly vertically, but at about 75 to 80 degrees from horizontal. It should also circle the line in one direction or the other. As it slows, it will spin in a helix pattern before flattening out to horizontal again.

> WHAT'S GOING ON? This experiment demonstrates two principles: precession (a spinning object orbits its axis) and angular momentum (a circular-moving force that happens because the mass of the wheel is mainly in its rim). A bicycle gains stability as it goes faster—because it maintains the angular momentum of the wheels.

QUESTION THIS!

• Why is it hard to ride a bike extremely slowly?

• What's the relationship between this experiment and a "sleeping" yo-yo?

"So that's why a bike keels over when you slow down . . ."
—Nick

BIKE WHEEL GYROSCOPE
PART 2

Feel the force!

ANGULAR MOMENTUM, INERTIA, VELOCITY, FRICTION, TORQUE

HOW LONG IT TAKES
fifteen minutes

WHAT YOU NEED
a BMX bicycle wheel or other small solid-axle bike wheel with pegs attached, as in the first Bike Wheel Gyroscope experiment, page 6
a swivel chair
a partner

You're used to the idea that pushing the pedals on a bike powers the bike. Here's what happens when a bicycle wheel is used to power you as you sit on a swivel chair instead of the seat of the bike. For comparison, sit on a chair that doesn't swivel.

WHAT TO DO

1 **SIT IN A SWIVEL** chair.

2 **HOLD THE WHEEL** by its pegs. Place the wheel in a vertical position.

3 **HAVE YOUR PARTNER** set the wheel spinning.

4 **TURN THE WHEEL** so that it spins horizontally. What happens?

5 **NOW TURN** the still-spinning wheel over so that it's spinning in the opposite direction. What happens?

6 **NOW HOLD** the spinning wheel vertically. What happens?

> **WHAT'S GOING ON?** Torque is a principle of a spinning object, a force that keeps it turning in a horizontal plane. This is what turns you as the angular momentum of the wheel is maintained by the spin. (This is the odd force you feel as the wheel causes your whole body to turn in the chair.) When you turn the wheel over, the force reverses direction. But holding the wheel vertically will not turn the chair.

QUESTION THIS!

How does it feel to hold the spinning wheel horizontally when you're not in a swivel chair?

"You can feel a force pulling at you."
—Adriana

WALKING ON EGGS

Distribute your weight evenly ... then wait.

HOW LONG IT TAKES
one hour

WHAT YOU NEED
at least four one-dozen cartons of eggs
(the cartons preferably made of varied
materials: cardboard, plastic, Styrofoam)
a curb or low stool
your bare feet
optional crutches, a cane, a railing, a
staircase with a bannister

Do you feel like you're walking on eggshells around us? You could be. Eggshells are specially made to protect what's inside—and so are egg cartons. See how much pressure they can take.

"Cracks are forming!"
—Dylan

1 HERE'S THE IDEAL setup; try to replicate it or to create a similar situation.

A porch stoop with a railing on each side. Place the open egg carton on the sidewalk and stand on the lowest step. Holding the railings, gently place your bare feet atop the eggs. Carefully shift your weight until you are standing squarely on top of the eggs, then let go of the railings.

2 REPEAT WITH the other two boxes of eggs, being careful to do it the same way each time.

> **WHAT TO EXPECT** You are highly likely to break or crack some eggs, but one package type may triumph over the others in terms of cushioning effect.

> **WHAT'S HAPPENING?** Different materials respond in various degrees to the weight of your body atop the eggs.

QUESTION THIS!

• What would happen if you closed the cover of the egg carton before standing on it?

• How well would the box cushion the eggs if you just jumped on them or stood on them without taking the trouble to distribute your weight evenly?

• Does it make a difference whether the smaller ends of the eggs are turned up or down?

• How would you design an egg box that would do a better job of cushioning the eggs?

MAKE YOUR OWN LIFE JACKET

What would you do to stay afloat if you somehow fell in the water wearing clothes? Lifesavers learn to take off jeans or other pants in the water, to tie the ankles together in a big overhand knot, zip the jeans, and "inflate them" by filling them with water. Try this, then put the ankle knot behind your head and put your head through the legs to create a life vest. Why do you think filling the jeans with water allows them to float?

NOTE OF CAUTION
This is not an approved floating device.
(But it sure could help in an emergency!)

FROZEN BOUNCE

Does temperature affect bounce?

>> **HOW LONG IT TAKES**
three hours (including freezing time)

>> **WHAT YOU NEED**
two tennis balls
a freezer
a wall, basketball hoop pole, or stepladder
to drop ball from (we used a ladder)
chalk or string (we used "flag" tape ties,
just because they were handy) for mea-
suring the wall, pole, or stepladder
a metal tape measure

W hether it's reaching new heights or sticking closer to Earth, many different factors determine a ball's bounce. In this experiment, you'll look at conditions that could affect how much a ball will bounce. Once you've analyzed the conditions here, create some new ball drops: wet vs. dry; inflated vs. not so full—whatever you can think of!!

WHAT TO DO

1 PLACE A TENNIS ball in the freezer for at least two hours.

2 USE YOUR TAPE measure and chalk to mark out measurements on the wall, pole, or ladder. You can do this as you bounce the ball, using a different color chalk for each ball, or draw measurement markings on the wall ahead of time and record each ball's bounces in a notebook.

3 BOUNCE THE unfrozen tennis ball and see how high it bounces. In doing this, establish how you will bounce the ball, from what height, so that you can replicate the technique with the frozen ball. Bounce the unfrozen tennis ball at least ten times and record the measurements.

4 REPEAT with the frozen tennis ball.

> **WHAT TO EXPECT** One of the balls will bounce higher than the other.

> **WHAT'S HAPPENING?** When a material is frozen, its molecules contract, becoming more dense and causing it to become less flexible.

QUESTION THIS!

• How would your results change if you froze the tennis ball for longer?

• What difference does the surface on which you're bouncing the ball make?

• What difference does the height from which you bounce the ball make?

• What difference does the force with which you bounce the ball make?

BONUS:
BASKETBALL
BALL BOOST

Place a tennis ball on top of a basketball and let them both drop. What happens?

WHAT TO EXPECT The tennis ball will bounce surprisingly high.

WHAT'S HAPPENING? The basketball is heavier and lower, so it hits the ground first and bounces back up, hitting the tennis ball and transferring its momentum to the smaller ball, so the tennis ball goes higher than it would on its own.

"Whoa!"
—Brandon

DIET COKE vs. COKE
FLOATING SMACKDOWN

Which one floats?

CONCEPTS

BUOYANCY, DENSITY

HOW LONG IT TAKES
five minutes

WHAT YOU NEED
two cans of the same kind of soda, one diet and one regular
a container of water, such as an aquarium, a bathtub, a large pot or bucket

Will it float? A popular TV show asked this question, before dropping all sorts of items into containers of water. The audience and celebrities made predictions—and the outcomes were frequently surprising. Try that—and try this! When it comes to buoyancy, it can be tricky to hypothesize about what will and won't float.

1

WHAT TO DO

PLACE BOTH CANS of soda in the water. Observe what happens.

>> **WHAT TO EXPECT** One can should float and one should sink.

>> **WHAT'S GOING ON?** The regular soda has about ten teaspoons (50 mL) of sugar, with a density greater than that of water—more matter packed into a smaller space. But the diet soda has artificial sweetener, which is sweeter than sugar, so that less is required to make the sweet taste. The diet soda is less dense, so it floats.

QUESTION THIS!

• Does this work with other flavors of soda?

• What about other kinds of drinks with artificial sweeteners, such as iced tea?

BONUS:
RAINBOW
IN A JAR

Use light corn syrup, olive oil, Dawn dishwashing liquid, rubbing alcohol, and water. Determine which is most dense (and will sink to the bottom), which is least dense (and will rise to the top), and how the layers between will organize themselves, according to their density. Then use food coloring to color them each according to their density in order to create a rainbow. Finally, pour equal amounts of each liquid into the jar to test your density prediction.

ICE-SKATER EFFECT

Try a skater's spin—without ice.

CONCEPTS

INERTIA, ANGULAR MOMENTUM, FRICTION, VELOCITY

HOW LONG IT TAKES
fifteen minutes (including assembly time)

WHAT YOU NEED
two two-pound (.9-kg) hand weights
a swivel chair

Have you seen an ice-skater spin, bringing her hands in and out to increase her motion? This is what you're doing—without ice skates! As you bring your hands and arms (and weights) closer to your body, you move mass closer to the vertical axis of your rotation. You can use this information to speed up or slow your spin.

WHAT TO DO

1 SIT in the swivel chair.

2 HOLD THE WEIGHTS IN your hands and start to turn.

3 HOLD THE WEIGHTS AT chest level and open your arms to the side, with your elbows slightly bent. Now bend your elbows more and pull the weights in to your chest together. Continue this motion—in and out with the weights—to see how it affects your spin.

> **GLITCH?** The weights and your arm action don't get you moving? Start yourself with your feet, and then start the motion.

> **NOTE ABOUT SPINNING** Spotting is something dancers learn to do when they spin to keep from getting dizzy and to stay in control. Pick a spot on the wall, and as you spin, look for that spot, turning your head quickly to get to it.

> **WHAT TO EXPECT** The tighter, smaller motion (with the elbows bent all the way as you bring the weights to your chest) should increase your spin.

> **WHAT'S GOING ON?** In a spin, you reach a balance between inertia (no motion) and friction (in which motion slows). You spin faster when you pull your hands and the weights in, because you pull mass toward the center of the spin (its vertical axis).

QUESTION THIS!

• What part of the motion slows you down the most?

• How long can you keep spinning using the weights?

• Does the weight of the weights make a difference?

• Does the weight of the person doing the experiment change the outcome?

"That's weird!"
—Adriana

HOVER BALLOON

Ready for liftoff?

CONCEPTS

AERODYNAMICS, JET PROPULSION, AIR PRESSURE, HYDROFOILS

> **HOW LONG IT TAKES**
> thirty minutes to an hour

> **WHAT YOU NEED**
> CD
> balloon
> soda bottle cap
> drill
> hot glue gun and glue sticks
> tabletop or smooth floor

What's a hovercraft? It's a vehicle that blows an air cushion under itself to produce lift. As the vehicle is propelled forward, it floats above the surface—land, sea, or your tabletop.

QUESTION THIS!

• How could you improve the way these hover balloons work?

WHAT TO DO

1 DRILL a hole in the center of a soda bottle cap.

2 HOT-GLUE the bottle cap to the CD, centering it over the hole in the center of the CD.

3 BLOW UP THE BALLOON and, while pinching the neck closed, stretch the neck of the balloon over the bottle cap.

4 SET THE CD on the table or floor and release the balloon.

> WHAT TO EXPECT The hover balloon will scoot around the tabletop.

> WHAT'S GOING ON? The air inside the balloon releases down out of the balloon and creates a cushion of air under the CD, which moves around because the air cushion is uneven.

> GLITCH? This is a little tricky, but we got the hang of it and you will, too. It's easier if you stretch the neck of the balloon before trying to fit it over the bottle cap. You can also have a friend fit the balloon on the bottle cap for you while you hold the balloon closed.

RACING ROCKET BALLOONS

Fun that goes *pfffft*

CONCEPTS

JET PROPULSION, AERODYNAMICS, MECHANICS, FRICTION

HOW LONG IT TAKES
one hour

WHAT YOU NEED
wire or string
balloons
hockey tape, electrical
tape, or another cloth tape
plastic straws
optional: permanent
markers

This is fun to do with a few other people, so you can race your balloons.

RACING ROCKET BALLOONS
(CONTINUED)

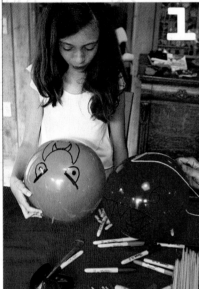

1 INFLATE A BALLOON. If you want, draw a face or wings or messages on your balloon.

2 USE TWO PIECES of tape to attach a straw to it. Attach the straw so that its ends are toward the top and bottom of the balloon. Now let the balloon deflate.

TO SET UP THE RACE COURSE:

3 MEASURE THE distance you want your balloon to travel. For example, if you want it to rocket across the room, measure the room. Then cut a piece of wire or string that length. Attach one end of it to the wall at the other end of the room or to a piece of furniture.

4 THREAD THE LOOSE end of the wire through the straw on your balloon, starting at the top and ending at the bottom.

5 ATTACH THE END of the wire to a railing or chair back in front of you. (See picture 6.)

6 ALL TOGETHER, blow up your balloons and pinch the neck to hold the air in.

7 READY, SET, LET GO! At the signal, let go of your balloon and let it fly along the wire.

WHAT TO EXPECT Your balloon may—or may not—zip along the wire or string. It depends on the angle and length of the "race course" and the positioning and length of the straw.

WHAT'S GOING ON? As the air shoots out of the balloon, it propels the balloon along the wire or string.

GLITCH? Balloons don't go? Consider changing the position of the straw, or using a longer or shorter piece of straw.

QUESTION THIS!

- What difference do the angle and length of the wire make?
- What shape balloon works best?
- What amount of air works best?
- What works best: small or large balloons? Oblong or long ones?
- What works best: wire or string?

BONUS:
SKEWER YOUR BALLOON

Try poking a skewer (metal or bamboo like ours) through a balloon. Blow up a balloon and knot it. Insert the point of the skewer next to the knot, through the balloon, and out the other end where there's a dark spot on the balloon's skin. (With thanks to Jarrett Nunes for the tip.)

"The skewer can go through the balloon because the polymer (balloon material) wraps around the skewer, which makes the air not leak out."
—Jarrett

CREDITS

Acknowledgments

Our Models: Aaliyah, Abigail, Adriana, Allison, Ariel, Bailey, Brandon, Caitlyn, Cole, Doug, Dylan, Emily, Isaac, Janelle, Jarrett, Jason, Jen, Justin, Lori, Luke, Mae, Marco, Nick, Nikitha, Niyanna, Patsy, Priyanka, Serenity, Sossi, Stephanie, Trijon, Wyatt

Special thanks to Tina Kiniry at the John Casablancas Modeling Agency

All photographs shot on location by Matthew Rakola

Published by the National Geographic Society

John M. Fahey, *Chairman of the Board and Chief Executive Officer*
Declan Moore, *Executive Vice President; President, Publishing and Travel*
Melina Gerosa Bellows, *Executive Vice President; Chief Creative Officer, Books, Kids, and Family*

Prepared by the Book Division

Hector Sierra, *Senior Vice President and General Manager*
Nancy Laties Feresten, *Senior Vice President, Kids Publishing and Media*
Jennifer Emmett, *Vice President, Editorial Director, Kids Books*
Eva Absher-Schantz, *Design Director, Kids Publishing and Media*
Jay Sumner, *Director of Photography, Kids Publishing and Media*
R. Gary Colbert, *Production Director*
Jennifer A. Thornton, *Director of Managing Editorial*

Staff for This Book

Priyanka Lamichhane, *Project Editor*
Angela Modany, *Assistant Editor*
Eva Absher-Schantz, *Art Director*
Lori Epstein, *Senior Photo Editor*
Itzhack Shelomi, *Designer*
Ariane Szu-Tu, *Editorial Assistant*
Paige Towler, *Editorial Intern*
Sanjida Rashid and Rachel Kenny, *Design Production Assistants*
Margaret Leist, *Photo Assistant*
Grace Hill, *Associate Managing Editor*
Joan Gossett, *Production Editor*
Lewis R. Bassford, *Production Manager*
Susan Borke, *Legal and Business Affairs*

Production Services

Phillip L. Schlosser, *Senior Vice President*
Chris Brown, *Vice President, NG Book Manufacturing*
George Bounelis, *Senior Production Manager*
Nicole Elliott, *Director of Production*
Rachel Faulise, *Manager*
Robert L. Barr, *Manager*

The National Geographic Society is one of the world's largest nonprofit scientific and educational organizations. Founded in 1888 to "increase and diffuse geographic knowledge," the Society's mission is to inspire people to care about the planet. It reaches more than 400 million people worldwide each month through its official journal, *National Geographic*, and other magazines; National Geographic Channel; television documentaries; music; radio; films; books; DVDs; maps; exhibitions; live events; school publishing programs; interactive media; and merchandise. National Geographic has funded more than 10,000 scientific research, conservation and exploration projects and supports an education program promoting geographic literacy.

For more information, please visit nationalgeographic .com, call 1-800-NGS LINE (647-5463), or write to the following address:
  National Geographic Society
  1145 17th Street N.W.
  Washington, D.C. 20036-4688 U.S.A.

Visit us online at nationalgeographic.com/books

For librarians and teachers: ngchildrensbooks.org

More for kids from National Geographic: kids.nationalgeographic.com

For information about special discounts for bulk purchases, please contact National Geographic Books Special Sales: ngspecsales@ngs.org

For rights or permissions inquiries, please contact National Geographic Books Subsidiary Rights: ngbookrights@ngs.org

Dollar Tree edition ISBN: 978-1-4263-2381-2

Printed in the U.S.A.
15/KG/1